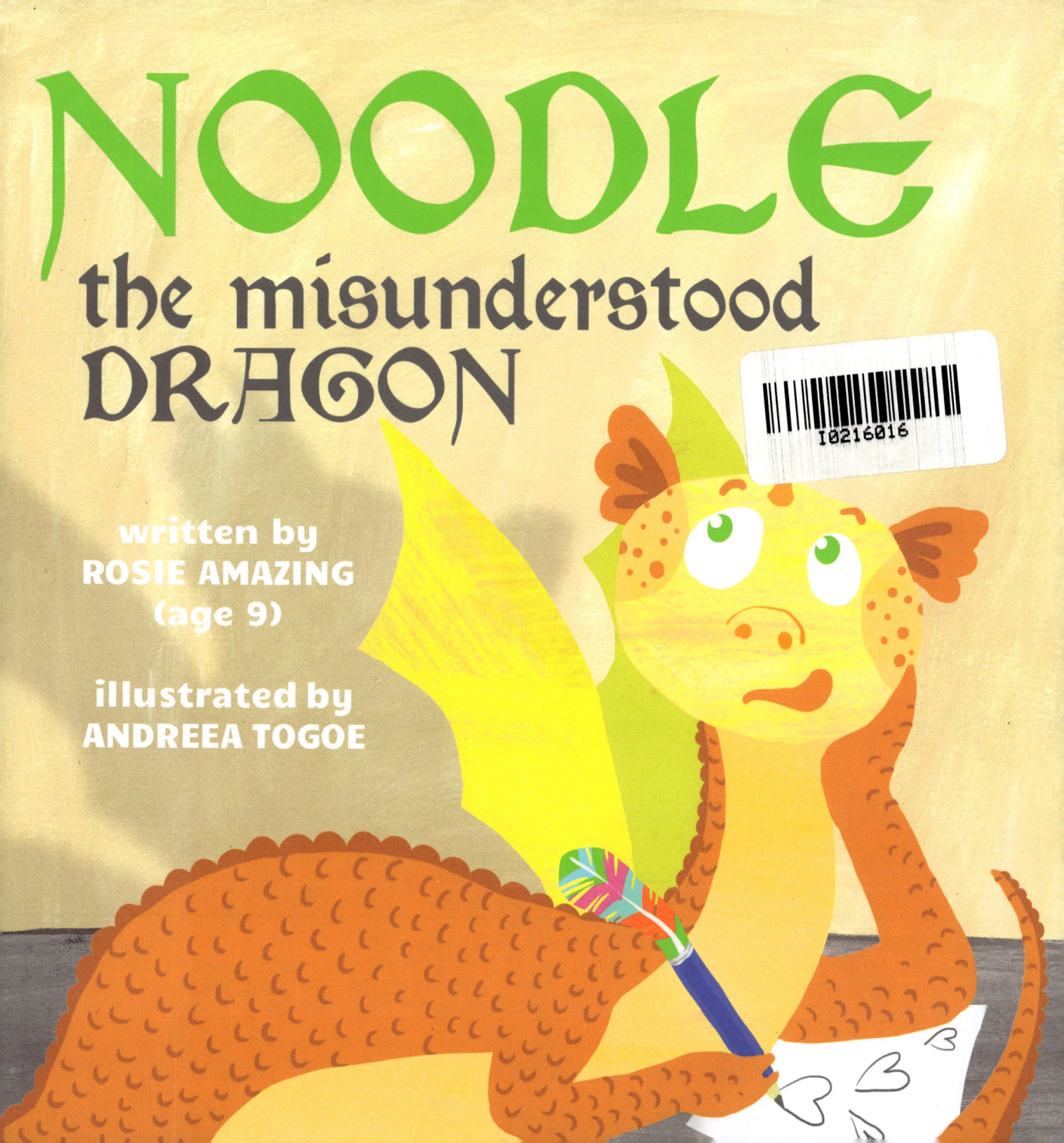

Once upon a time, in Medieval Times, there was a dragon Named Noodle.

"Hi! I'm noodle!" he said.

But Noodle had no friends because everyone thought he was super-dangerous.

One day when Noodle was waking up from his nap, he poked his head up and something blew in the wind, slapping him in the face.

"Mmmmfffmmfffm!" Noodle spluttered with his mouth full of poster.

Noodle sneezed the poster off his face.

"ACHOOOO!"

Flames streamed from his mouth and nostrils.

Once Noodle snorted the flames back inside his nose, he looked down at the poster. Upon it was a picture of Princess Delilah.

"Delilah?" Noodle said with glee. "The kindest princess ever? I want to play with her! But how can I possibly get to her when all the villagers are afraid of me?"

Noodle came up with a plan. One night, he snuck stealthily into the castle. He wrote a note with a pencil and eraser. He couldn't spell too well, but he did his best. Then he carried the note in his mouth towards Princess Delilah's bedroom.

"I'll slip this note under her door," Noodle whispered to himself. "I'll invite her for a little ride to my cave, and we can have a little tea party!"

Princess Dellah found the note, and also Noodle, who had been patiently waiting in the hall.

"I heard you are the kindest princess, right?" Noodle asked.

"Ooooh yeah, I am," the princess replied. "But I'm a little scared of dragons."

"You don't need to be!" Noodle said earnestly. "I'm friendly. Would you like to have a tea party with me?"

"Yay!" cheered the princess.

The princess hopped on the dragon's back, and Noodle zoomed through the sky towards his cave.

"Yyyyyewawww!" the prince yawned when he woke up that morning.

The prince fumbled out of bed, walked down the hall and tripped on something.

"Whoa! Ooof! Ugh!" he cried. "That royally hurt!"

He got down and his hands and knees and found a note...

I took your princess so we can do stuff.

Love Noodle the Mustard Dragon

Noodle had tried to sign the letter *Misunderstood* Dragon, but he didn't know how to spell *misunderstood*, so he accidentally wrote *mustard*.

"UH-OH!" The prince freaked. "Delilah has been kidnapped by a mustard dragon! NO! Now the princess is going to get eaten!"

The prince went so crazy, he ran up the walls, ran up the ceiling, he ran up EVERYTHING.

He suddenly stopped. "Wait, I need to tell my dad this."

Then he fell.

"Oof! Ouchie!"

Then he barged out the door.

"Dad! WAKE UUUUUP!" the prince screamed in the king's ear.

"AAAH! WHAT IS IT?" the king yelped, sitting up and looking around. "Oh, it's only you."

"My sister got kidnapped by a dragon!" he screamed.

"A DRAGON?" shrieked the king. "But her wedding is in one week!"

"I KNOW!" the prince said warily. "We need to do something!"

"Son, I think you're old enough to battle that dragon! I mean, lots of other princes have done this kind of thing and succeeded. Even little wimpy princes."

"Okay," the prince said nervously. "I will find Princess Delilah!"

The prince quickly read all the books in the royal library and frantically drew a map of all the places he just read about. He put on some armour and grabbed a sword.

He followed the map and found a sunflower dragon.

"Are you the mustard dragon?" the prince asked. "Did you kidnap the princess?"

"Me?" asked the sunflower dragon. "Why, I only eat plants. Not princesses. See? Nom nom nom."

Then the prince found an orchid dragon. And a butterfly dragon. And two crystal dragons. Even a bamboo dragon who was busy meditating. Then a rose dragon who was so offended, she hurled thorns into the prince's butt.

None of the dragons had even heard of Princess Delilah.

Where was the mustard dragon?

The prince was running out of dragons. But then he spotted Noodle having a tea party with Princess Delilah in a cave.

"ARGH!" the prince said, charging into the cave, trying to sound scary.

"Oh hi, brother!" Delilah said cheerily.

"Are you a guest?" asked Noodle.

"NO!" the prince screamed. "I'm here to rescue Princess Delilah!"

"Rescue me?"

"Yes! I just saw that dragon try to sprinkle sugar on you so he can eat you!"

"Not on ME!" the princess giggled. "He was sprinkling sugar on my tea!"

"But he's the mustard dragon!"

"MISUNDERSTOOD DRAGON!" the princess laughed. "Oh brother, you are so weird!"

The prince blinked. He had never been so embarrassed.

A week later, was the royal wedding, and Noodle was invited! He was so excited to be included, he completely forgot about the embarrassing misunderstanding.

Like Rosie's Books?

Support Rosie by leaving a positive review on Amazon or GoodReads.

Keep up-to-date by following us on Instagram:

https://www.instagram.com/annelidpress/

Copyright © 2025 by Annelid Press
ISBN: 978-1-990292-53-8

All rights reserved. Published by Annelid Press. No part of this publication may be reproduced, stored in a retrieval system or transmitted, in any form or by any means, without the prior written permission of Annelid Press.